# Giving Birth to

*Anxiety*

## The Hope to Overcome Postpartum Anxiety

Anjelica Williams

*Giving Birth to Anxiety*
Copyright © 2025 Anjelica Williams
All rights reserved.

No part of this book may be reproduced or transmitted in any form or by any means, electronic, mechanical, including photocopying, recording, or by an information storage and retrieval system for the purpose of profit making without permission in writing from the author.

Published by 100X Publishing, Olympia, Washington
www.100xpublishing.com

Scriptures marked NLT are taken from the HOLY BIBLE, NEW LIVING TRANSLATION, Copyright© 1996, 2004, 2007 by Tyndale House Foundation. Used by permission of Tyndale House Publishers, Inc., Carol Stream, Illinois 60188. All rights reserved.

The ESV® Bible (The Holy Bible, English Standard Version®), © 2001 by Crossway, a publishing ministry of Good News Publishers. ESV Text Edition: 2025.

Paperback ISBN: 979-8-9929258-1-4

# Dedication

First and foremost, I dedicate this book to my husband—my rock and my best friend. Thank you for your unwavering love, encouragement, and for always believing in me, even when I struggled to believe in myself. Your presence has been a steady light through every step of this journey.

To my two incredible boys: you have pushed me, challenged me, and inspired me to become a greater version of myself. You are my motivation, my joy, and my deepest pride. I love you both with all that I am.

And to my Lord and Savior, Jesus Christ: You saved me, and You continue to save me every single day. All glory, honor, and power belong to You. Amen.

# Contents

Introduction ............................................................................. 7
1: Prep Time .......................................................................... 11
2: "Oops, I Drew Blood..." .................................................. 15
3: "Fight or Flight" ............................................................... 21
4: Everyone Needs a Jen ..................................................... 29
5: How Did I Get Here? ...................................................... 35
6: Resisting the Real Enemy .............................................. 41
7: The Floor Became Holy Ground ................................... 45
8: Here We Go...Again ........................................................ 49
9: Redemption Birth ............................................................ 55
10: Learning Is Not Linear .................................................. 59
11: Progress Over Perfection .............................................. 65
Real Moms' Stories .............................................................. 67
Tools for Hope ...................................................................... 75
Author Bio ............................................................................. 83

# Introduction

There's something to be said about being young and naive—you don't know what you don't know. Like many expectant mothers, I had my own ideas of what motherhood would be like. As the oldest of three, I thought having younger siblings was God's way of preparing me early. I'd spent years watching my mom, mentally taking notes, assuming that one day I'd be ready when it was my turn. But none of my close friends had children at the time, and truthfully, I had no clue. No amount of babysitting or observing could have prepared me for what hit me the moment I gave birth to my first son.

I did what I thought I was supposed to do—I signed up for every hospital class I could find, followed all the Instagram "new mommy" pages, and clung to the sweet, encouraging notes from my baby shower like they were a guidebook. I truly believed I was ready.

But here's the thing: *nothing prepares you for that first moment with your baby.*

If your moment was everything you thought it would be—I genuinely envy you. Mine was anything but. It wasn't warm or fuzzy. It was raw, overwhelming, and not at all what I expected.

> In the moment that I gave birth to my son, I was simultaneously giving birth to anxiety in my life.

The room was spinning, and I was trying to make sense of what had just happened. I had just brought a human into the world. But instead of euphoria, I felt terrified. And then came the guilt.

Whether you had a scheduled C-section, an emergency C-section, a natural home birth, or even an accidental one (more on that later), chances are things didn't go exactly how you wrote them out in your birth plan. Oh, those birth plans!

Sometimes life throws you a curveball so wild you never even saw it coming. My journey with postpartum anxiety was exactly that—a life-altering curveball that hit me fast and hard. And as I walked through it, one overwhelming thought kept coming back to me: *there has to be a purpose for this kind of pain.*

Maybe you picked up this book because, like me, you've typed desperate Google searches like "symptoms of postpartum anxiety" or "why can't I stop worrying about my baby?" Or maybe the term *postpartum anxiety* is brand new to you, but the title of this book sparked something—a curiosity, a question, a hope for answers to the constant worrying, sleeplessness, and restlessness that seem to have taken over your life as a mother.

Whatever brought you here, I want you to know how thankful I am that you picked up this book. My hope in sharing my story is that you'll find the courage to ask for help, the hope to keep going, and the peace that comes with knowing you are not alone.

Before I pour my heart out over the next several pages, let me say this: I am not a doctor, therapist, or medical professional of any kind. I'm just a mom—though trust me, there's nothing *just* about that—who went through some 'ish' and felt called to share my story. This isn't a guidebook or a how-to. It's not filled with clinical terms or textbook answers. This is simply my truth—raw, unfiltered, and straight from the trenches of new motherhood. I'm sharing it in hopes that it connects with someone out there, encourages a weary soul, or maybe even helps a fellow mama feel a little less alone. If it blesses you, then every word will have been worth it. Okay, now that we've gotten that out of the way...

I will tell you, this book was birthed from a place of deep pain, but in the very same breath, from a place of unshakable hope. I spent countless sleepless nights searching for answers and found very few. As Toni Morrison once said, "If there's a book that you want to read, but it hasn't been written yet, then you must write it."

So, this is the book I needed. And maybe, just maybe, it's the one you need too.

# CHAPTER ONE

*Prep Time*

> "Pregnancy is a process that invites you to surrender to the unseen force behind all life" —Judy Ford

If you were to have met me in 2017, I would have been 28, happily married to my wonderful husband Mason for two and a half years, and getting ready to meet our first child that June—a boy.

A little backstory first.

I guess you could say I've always been the type to see the glass as half full. Optimism was second nature to me, not something I had to force. If someone around me was having a bad day, I felt almost morally responsible to make it better—like it was my personal mission to shift the energy in the room. I didn't know it at the time, but I lived for picking others up.

For ten years, I poured that same heart into my work as a hairdresser. My job was so much more than cutting or coloring hair; it was about connection. My clients became friends, even family in some ways. I wasn't successful because I was the best stylist in town, I was successful because I genuinely cared. I listened. I remembered birthdays. I noticed when someone's smile didn't quite reach their eyes. And I did everything I could to make sure that by the time they got out of my chair, they were carrying just a little less of whatever was weighing them down. It brought me joy to bring others joy.

I was also blessed with a loving, supportive family. My parents gave my siblings and me a wonderful childhood filled with encouragement, laughter, and stability. I knew what it was to feel seen and safe.

Up until that point in my life, I hadn't really struggled with anxiety. Sure, I'd get nervous before big events or spiral a little when I had a headache and convinced myself it was something fatal (recovering hypochondriac, right here). But even in those moments, I always managed to talk myself down. My inner monologue was strong and steady. *Everything is going to be okay. Don't think, just do. God's got this.* And honestly, that mindset worked. Life had its ups and downs, but I never really felt stuck in fear or worry. I knew how to move through it.

Then came the day I found out I was pregnant.

It was one of the most joy-filled moments of my life. I remember staring at the little plus sign on the test and immediately rushing to my husband's job because I couldn't contain my excitement. We hugged, we cried, we dreamed together. The nine months stretched out before us was like this beautiful unknown, and we couldn't wait to meet our baby.

To my surprise and deep gratitude, pregnancy was kind to me. I felt good physically, and emotionally I was over the moon. I took it seriously too, preparing for labor like it was an Olympic event. Signing up for every class the hospital offered, I followed all the right social media accounts and even joined a prenatal group.

The pre-natal group my OBGYN suggested was made up of six other expectant mothers, all due around the same time. We saw each other once a month, did our check-ups together, and built a little community around shared anticipation and excitement.

Looking back, it's clear that I threw myself into the preparation—reading, learning, planning—because I wanted to do everything "right." I was determined to be ready.

But what I didn't do was prepare for *after*.

I thought labor was the mountain, and once I climbed it—once the baby was here—everything else would fall into place. I never stopped to think about what life might look like in those blurry, emotional, sleep-deprived days to follow. I didn't consider how drastically everything would shift or how I would shift.

Despite all the education, all the books, the classes, and conversations, I was wildly, painfully unprepared for the reality of postpartum. What came after the birth of my son shook me in ways I never expected. It cracked open parts of me I didn't even know existed.

So if you're still with me, buckle up.

What I'm about to share isn't always pretty. It's not sugarcoated, and it's certainly not filtered through some Instagram-worthy motherhood lens. But it's real. And if you've ever felt like you were the only one struggling behind the scenes, this part is for you.

Let me take you on the journey of what happened *after the birth.*

## CHAPTER TWO

*"Oops, I Drew Blood..."*

"Being a Mother is learning about strengths you didn't know you had, and dealing with fears you didn't know existed."
—Nishan Panwar

I finally made it to my due date and still no baby! Oh the anticipation! Did I mention I was impatient? I tried every natural remedy I could find on Pinterest to make labor happen. Walking, teas, essential oils, bouncing on a yoga ball until I was sure he was just going to fall out. Still no luck. I was determined to try a drug-free, intervention-free labor as long as I could. But at 41 weeks, there was pressure from my OBGYN to start the induction process, so I trustingly went along with what was recommended.

There was very little talk about induction in the classes I attended, so I really had no idea what was coming next nor how to prepare. The OBGYN recommended the Foley Bulb, or "Balloon Induction," so that's the route I took. I went home with the ballon in place and let it do its thing. Hours and hours went by with no contractions, no water broken, nothing. The doctor told me to come in at midnight that night so we could start on Pitocin, which I really did not want to do. But at this point I was tired of waiting and so eager to meet my son, so my husband and I packed our hospital bags and headed over that night. *This is it*, or so I thought.

Around 2 a.m. the nurses started me on Pitocin. It was slow going at first, but the contractions started to pick up a little in the early morning. A doctor came in to check me, and to my surprise I was only three centimeters dilated! So, they left me to do my thing. Another three to four hours went by, and the contractions picked up but were not intense. The doctor comes in again to check on me, and I had barely budged—now at four centimeters. I couldn't believe it!

At this point I had been up for over 40 hours and exhaustion was starting to take a toll, but I was determined to keep going. A few more hours went by with barley any progress. *What's a girl got to do to get a baby around here?* I remember turning to my husband and saying, "I guess this is when I get the epidural."

As we waited for the anesthesiologist to come, it was like I entered a twilight zone. Everything became more intense, my heart was beating out of my chest, and for the first time I felt utterly afraid of what was to come next. A young lady walked through the door and was letting me know everything that she was going to do, but honestly I don't remember a thing of what was said. My racing mind wouldn't quiet down, and fear started to creep in like a slow leaking faucet. All the what ifs flooded my mind like a tsunami.

So there I am, hunched over, gripping my husband's hand as tightly as I could, trying to steady myself. The nurse gently reminds me to take a deep breath in—and then *OUCH*. I know some women say they barely feel the epidural needle, and others say it didn't hurt at all. But for me? It was an intense, sharp pain in my lower back that didn't let up. My whole body was rigid with fear, and even though the nurse kept coaching me to breathe and relax, I couldn't. I was trying—desperately—but I was too tense, too overwhelmed.

And then, the anesthesiologist uttered the words that still bring a lump to my throat:

> *"Oops, I drew blood. Looks like we're going to have to do that again."*

*Excuse me? Again?* I was stunned. Frozen. That moment was the first time I truly felt like I had lost all control of what was happening to me and my body. I felt like a passenger in my own experience—powerless, terrified, and trapped. With shaking hands and a racing heart, I hunched over again, even more terrified the second time. She went in once more. It hurt just as much, but at least this time it worked—or so I thought.

As the epidural started to take effect, a strange, unsettling numbness crawled across my body. I was finally able to close my eyes for what felt like a brief moment—just enough time to hope for some relief—before a contraction ripped me back awake. Something wasn't right. The epidural had only taken on my right side, leaving the left side of my body to feel every contraction. I was stunned. I had been awake for nearly two days straight, and now I was supposed to keep laboring with nothing left in the tank—no sleep, no fuel, and absolutely no peace.

At some point, the nurses gave me something to help numb my left side. I still don't know exactly what it was, but it worked—almost too well. Within minutes, the numbness started to rise up my torso. It crept into my chest, then down my left arm, and that is when I *lost it*. I went from being anxious to full-blown panic mode. I couldn't breathe. My thoughts were racing. My heart was pounding. I felt like I was disappearing into my own fear. Nurses rushed in, and a doctor followed, trying to calm me down. I heard them, but I couldn't come back to myself. On the outside, I was doing everything I could to appear okay, but on the inside I was screaming for someone to stop all of it, to make me feel safe again.

I wish I could say that the epidural made labor easier, but it didn't—not really. The pain didn't stop, and now I had the added burden of mistrust. I had lost faith in the people and medicine that were meant to care for me. The terror had settled deep into my mind and heart. Hours passed. The exhaustion never left. I was still in pain.

Finally, that evening, a doctor came in and broke my water to try to get things moving. And something *did* finally shift. Soon after, I was checked again. "You're at ten centimeters," the doctor said. "It's time to push."

Finally—*finally*—some good news.

Adrenaline took over, and I found a strength I didn't know I had. I pushed with everything in me—again and again, for 45 minutes. And then, just like that, Emmanuel Zion—my E.Z.—entered the world.

I looked at him and thought, *Everything is going to be okay now.*

Or at least, I *hoped* it would be.

# CHAPTER THREE

*"Fight or Flight"*

*"My anxiety doesn't come from thinking about the future, it's wanting to control it."* —Hugh Prather

When the doctors first placed E.Z. on my chest, something immediately felt wrong. His little body was completely limp, his skin an unsettling shade of deep purple, and the silence in the room was deafening. He wasn't crying—just still. I remember looking down at him, hoping for even the smallest sound or twitch, but he just lay there, motionless. The nurses and doctors moved quickly, their hands brisk and focused as they wiped him down and tried to stimulate him, urging him to breathe, to cry, to show any sign of life. But there was nothing—no gasp, no whimper, no cry.

My heart sank into a hollow space I didn't know existed. I was trying to stay present, trying to grasp what was happening, but it felt like I was watching everything through thick glass. I couldn't even speak; I was just frozen in disbelief, in fear, in helplessness. Before I could process the weight of what was unfolding, they lifted him off my chest and rushed him to the other side of the room. My body felt empty, cold, and exposed in a way I'd never experienced.

And then, finally, after what felt like an eternity, I heard him let out a big, gurgley cry—wet and raw and beautiful. I should have felt relief, and I did for a second, but soon after all I felt was exhaustion and fear again. I rested my head back against the pillow, tears running down the sides of my face, and thought to myself, *"I am not okay."* Because in that moment, despite the cry, despite the hope, I wasn't okay. I was scared, shaken to my core, and unsure of what was ahead.

The hours that followed felt like a blur, but also like time was crawling. After that moment—after hearing his cry and still not feeling okay—I found it almost impossible to ground myself. It was like my nervous system had been cracked wide open. Everything around me felt too loud, too bright, too much. Simple things—drinking water, answering a question, even just breathing—became mountains I had to scale. That first night, I didn't sleep at all. Not even for a minute. My body was still in shock, trembling uncontrollably, as if it hadn't yet realized that labor was over. My heart raced through the quiet darkness, and I couldn't stop replaying those first terrifying moments. Was he really okay? Was I? My thoughts spiraled and looped, tightening around my chest. I wanted to be present, to hold onto the joy of his birth, but my anxiety had taken the reins, and I couldn't seem to find the version of myself I had expected to be after giving birth. I felt like I was floating outside my body, watching myself try to mother, try to function, while deep inside I was unraveling.

My husband was by my side the whole time, doing everything he could to support me. He held my hand, brought me water, reminded me to breathe, and kept reassuring me that we were okay, that E.Z. was okay. He was patient and steady in a way I desperately needed, gently trying to help me make sense of what I was feeling. But no matter how hard I tried, I couldn't seem to explain what was happening inside me. It wasn't just fear, it was something deeper, more tangled. I felt like I was drowning in emotions I didn't have names for. When he asked how I was doing, all I could manage were vague answers like, "Something is very wrong," or "I don't know." But it was so much more than that. I wanted to open up, to tell him how scared I still was, how out of control I felt in my own skin, but the words just wouldn't come. It was like my mind and my mouth were disconnected, and I didn't know how to bridge the gap. All I knew was that something inside me had shifted, and I wasn't sure what or how.

The days that followed were some of the longest of my life. I went through the motions of caring for E.Z.—feeding him, holding him, changing him—but inside I felt like I was just barely holding it together. My body was still healing, sore and weak, but it was my mind that felt the most fragile. Every little sound E.Z. made jolted me into high alert. Every silence sent my thoughts spiraling. I couldn't relax, couldn't rest, couldn't shake the fear that something else might go wrong. My husband continued to be my anchor, staying up with me through the night, rubbing my back when I shook from anxiety, reminding me we were safe. I could see in his eyes how much he wanted to take the fear away from me. But this fear wasn't logical; it lived deep in my bones now.

There were moments I would sit and stare at the wall while E.Z. slept, feeling completely outside of myself. I knew I loved my son—fiercely—but I also felt disconnected, like I was watching our life from the outside. I remember one afternoon, sitting in the rocking chair with him asleep on my chest, and I suddenly realized I hadn't eaten all day. The basic needs I once met without a second thought now felt like monumental tasks. Showering, answering a text, even smiling—it all took effort. I was constantly on edge, bracing for something I couldn't name.

Prior to the birth of my son, I had never heard the term *postpartum anxiety*—only *postpartum depression*. I thought I knew what to expect: the baby blues, some crying, exhaustion, and mood swings. But nothing prepared me for what I actually experienced.

According to Healthline, postpartum anxiety can be described as "a constant worry that cannot be eased, feelings of dread about things you fear will happen, sleep disruption when your baby is sleeping peacefully, and racing thoughts." The physical symptoms include extreme fatigue, heart palpitations, hypertension, sweating, shaking, or trembling. I was feeling *every single one* of those symptoms—all at the same time.

You always hear that the first six weeks are the hardest with a newborn: learning how to breastfeed, waking up every few hours to feed or pump (or both), riding out hormonal crashes, managing baby blues, caring for cracked nipples, changing your own postpartum diapers, and the list goes on. Everyone told me these things were *normal,* just part of the experience. But inside, I felt completely undone.

In my mind, I wasn't connecting with the joy or happiness that's supposed to come with bringing home a new baby. And if, for a fleeting second, I did feel a moment of peace, it was instantly swallowed by overwhelming dread—the unshakable feeling that something terrible was going to happen. I couldn't leave my son's side. I was convinced that if I stepped away, even for a moment, something bad would happen to him. Then, I'd get upset with myself for struggling to do even the simplest things, like letting my husband take a feeding shift or stepping away to shower.

I was terrified, afraid my baby might die or that I might die from the sheer intensity of the anxiety and exhaustion. I worried that if I didn't get a grip on myself, I wouldn't be able to care for my baby the way he needed. I was averaging maybe two hours of sleep a day, if that. My body and mind were completely depleted, and my worry began turning into full-blown panic.

The scariest moment came one night when I couldn't sleep at all. My husband and baby were asleep next to me, but I couldn't even close my eyes. Worry-filled thoughts raged out of control, my heart was pounding, my hands were sweating, and I truly believed I was dying. I was gripped by fear so intense it felt physical—like I was coming out of my skin. And still, through it all, I had to keep going. I had to feed my son through cracked, bleeding nipples. I had to hold him through endless cluster feedings and try to decode every cry. But when he cried, it didn't feel like something I could respond to calmly; it felt like a five-alarm fire going off in my head. Everything inside me screamed that something was *wrong*, even when everyone else said this was normal newborn behavior.

One sleepless night turned into two. Then three. And by that point, I knew I needed help.

Six days after giving birth, I called my OB's office and scheduled an appointment. When I walked into her office, I sat down and just cried. *Hard.* I let everything pour out. The fear, the exhaustion, the guilt, the shame, the confusion—all of it. And instead of brushing it off, she looked at me with compassion and said, "Your body is in fight-or-flight mode. It's remembering the trauma from labor. It thinks it's still in danger."

This explanation changed everything. According to Merriam-Webster, *fight-or-flight* is "the instinctive physiological response to a threatening situation, which readies one to resist forcibly or run away." That was it—that's exactly how I felt. *Threatened.* On edge. Wanting to run. I finally had the words to describe what had been swallowing me whole.

And in that moment, for the first time, I felt a tiny bit of relief—not because everything was better but because someone *understood.* I wasn't broken. I was overwhelmed. I wasn't alone. I was in pain. And I had finally started to name it.

My doctor recommended that I join a postpartum support group hosted by the hospital. I wasn't sure what to expect, but something inside me clung to the idea with a quiet kind of hope. I didn't know if it would "fix" anything, but I was desperate for connection—for someone to tell me I wasn't losing my mind. A week later, I found myself standing in the hospital lobby, waiting for the group to begin. I felt like a kid on their first day of school—

nervous, uncertain, completely out of my element. *What will the class be like? What will we talk about? What if they think I'm crazy?* The questions swirled in my head as I bounced E.Z. gently in his car seat, trying to steady both him and myself.

Eventually, the facilitator appeared and welcomed me, along with five or six other moms, into a quiet room with chairs in a circle and soft lighting. As we each found a seat, I glanced around and slowly took everyone in. All of these women looked just like me—tired eyes, hair thrown up in messy buns, no makeup, babies fussing, arms full of swaddles and bottles. No one looked polished or put together. And for the first time in days, I didn't feel like I had to pretend.

Tears began rolling down my cheeks before I could stop them—not from sadness but from relief. These women weren't strangers anymore; they were proof I wasn't alone. I didn't have to explain the kind of exhaustion that leaves your bones aching or the quiet fear that hums beneath the surface of every feed. I knew instantly: *this is where I need to be.* A space where nothing had to be hidden. Where even if I couldn't yet speak all the words, I was surrounded by others who were living their own versions of the same storm.

# CHAPTER FOUR

## Everyone Needs a Jen

*"Walking with a friend in the dark is better than walking alone in the light."* —Helen Keller

Here's how Jen, one of the women in the Postpartum Support Group, described her experience with Postpartum Anxiety:

*"It started as my new normal. I wasn't sure if I was exhausted or depressed. It took me weeks to figure out it was both. I didn't feel any happiness, just obligation to a needy baby. And I knew that wasn't right. I couldn't understand why I couldn't feel joy at any level. I didn't even enjoy things I loved before I gave birth. I resented the tiny human who needed me so much. Angry at my useless nipples, feeling completely helpless and alone. It wasn't like the diaper commercials where parents instantly fall in love. I know without a doubt I loved my baby, but I didn't get that overwhelming rush of love when I looked at her like I expected I would have.*

*Something felt off, but I couldn't figure out what was wrong with me—why I was always crying, why I was always so sad. I wasn't happy to take care of my baby. It was something that I HAD to do, not something I*

wanted to do. I felt like a horrible mother. I remember talking to my step mother and asking her if this was normal. It wasn't. That's when I realized I should talk to someone, and that's when I started my postpartum group journey.

Finding out I wasn't alone or a horrible mother lifted a huge weight off my chest. Hearing other moms talk openly about what I was ashamed of allowed me to find acceptance and empowered me to talk about it too. Society makes us believe that if we aren't living in that perfect diaper commercial then we are wrong. But it allowed me to realize that life isn't like the diaper commercial for everyone, and to those few who get to actually experience it, I envy the hell out of you.

In order to cope, I began eating my feelings. I do not recommend this...but ice cream numbed the pain of what I was feeling, and double fudge brownie ice cream is delicious. I would binge eat lactation cookies and lie to myself that I was doing it for my baby. One cookie, maybe two, was a recommended serving, yet I would eat 12 and suffer the consequences of swollen painful boobs with too much milk. My husband was working hard to get me out of my funk too. He would celebrate the tiny wins in my day, like brushing my teeth or getting dressed. Having him acknowledge that these trivial tasks were huge accomplishments in my new normal made me feel good about myself and not a total failure. Once brushing my teeth became a regular occurrence and not an accomplishment, he added two things to my daily "to-do" list. He didn't care if I just put on another pair of pajamas, he was just proud of me for taking care of myself. Something I had completely forgotten how to do.

And then one day this new girl and her baby came to my postpartum group. When she spoke about her experiences, she spoke about Jesus and faith, and I did not think that we were going to be friends since I could not relate. But week after week she kept coming back, and the more she spoke, the more I became interested in her experiences, realizing we weren't so different. We were both women going through a negative experience and reaching out for help, so why couldn't that help come from me?

One day she asked me to lunch, and saying yes was the best decision I ever made. She was an amazing listener, she was understanding, and I could tell her anything because she didn't judge. That is what I needed. While my husband was my biggest supporter, he had useless nipples and couldn't relate. This girl new exactly what I was feeling and could talk to me openly about it. I could admit that breast feeding sucks and her response would be something like, 'Totally! I completely get it! It does suck! But it's so good for the babies, but formula is good too!'

No matter how I responded, I knew my answer couldn't be wrong because of how caring she was. It was my conversations with her that allowed me to fully open up and speak to others about how I was feeling. And if someone I spoke to judged me, I knew what I said was okay because it was how I was feeling. And Anjelica helped me figure that out. My feelings aren't wrong; they were valid because they were what I was feeling.

Anjelica has been a constant source of support and positivity, and I can call her at 3 a.m. crying and she drops what she's doing and talks me down. And I absolutely do the same for her. Having another mom have your back 24/7 is amazing and the only reason I have come so far in my postpartum journey."

I remember my first real interaction with Jen. It was my second time at the postpartum support group, and I had come in completely depleted—exhausted, stressed, and anxious after another sleepless night of breastfeeding. Just as the session was about to start, E.Z. began to fuss, hungry again. I reached into my bag, frantically searching for my breastfeeding cover, only to realize I must have left it at home. Panic rose in my chest. I didn't want to draw attention to myself.

Jen was sitting right next to me. I turned to her and asked, half-whispering, "Do you happen to have a cover I can borrow?" She looked at me without skipping a beat and said, "I have one you can use, but I just pull my boob out—no one cares here."

Something about the ease and honesty in her voice unlocked something in me. Her words were so casual, so confident, and somehow, so freeing. Of course I could feed my baby. *This* was a postpartum group. I wasn't on display; I was among women who *got it*. So, I did what she said: I pulled out my boob and fed my baby. And to my surprise, I didn't feel embarrassed or exposed. I felt *normal*. For the first time in my new mom journey, I felt like I belonged somewhere. Like maybe I didn't have to keep hiding how hard this was.

That group became so much more than just a weekly meeting, it became a lifeline. It was that way for many of us. The women who had been coming for a while made it their quiet mission to welcome new moms the moment they walked through the door. We all remembered that feeling—how terrifying and isolating those early days could be. So, when a mom came in, looking just as lost and sleep-deprived as we once had, we leaned in. We made space for her, just like others had made space for us.

In that circle, no one judged. When someone vented about cracked nipples or a husband who wasn't showing up in the way they needed or the resentment they felt toward family members who didn't understand, we didn't flinch. We listened. We nodded. We cried with them. We told them they weren't crazy. We reminded each other that this was the hardest thing most of us had *ever* done—and that we were doing it anyway.

I didn't know it at the time, but the group was keeping me afloat. On nights when anxiety had me wide-eyed and spiraling, or when I locked myself in the bathroom and cried on the floor, begging for a break, I would tell myself, *Just hold on until group. You're not alone. Jen will be there. Someone will understand.* And every week, without fail, Jen was there. Just like me. And that quiet consistency, that shared presence, saved me in ways I'm still so grateful for.

# CHAPTER FIVE

## *How Did I Get Here?*

*"Not everything that is faced can be changed, but nothing can be changed until it is faced." —James Baldwin*

If you have had a postpartum experience like me, I'm sure you asked yourself that very question, "How did I get here?" One month of postpartum anxiety turned into ten, and I felt like the woman who walked into that hospital room, excited and expectant to start this new chapter in life, was gone. I genuinely felt like I had lost myself. Looking into the mirror, through my dark circles and blood shot eyes, I was terrified at the person I saw looking back at me. Postpartum anxiety turned my light into darkness, my dancing into mourning, and my joy for life into utter fear for my future. The world that was once my oyster, now seemed like just a deep dark pit with no light to shine in, no hope.

You could say I was paralyzed by fear. I couldn't leave my son's side, and on the rare occasions I did step away—just to go to the grocery store alone or take a short walk—I couldn't enjoy a moment of it. My mind would spiral, flooded with worst-case scenarios of what might happen while I was gone. I could write an entire book filled with the intrusive thoughts that haunted me day and night— thoughts that robbed me of the joy I was supposed to feel as a new mother. But no one wants to talk about those thoughts because they're too heavy to hold, too painful to sort through—like an ocean too deep to cross.

If you know what I'm talking about, I'm so sorry. Even though they may be "just thoughts," they are anything but harmless. These terrifying, tormenting images that invade our minds—stealing our peace and poisoning our happiness—are the real reason many of us suffer in silence. I wished I could just stop thinking that something terrible was going to happen to my baby or to me. But it wasn't that simple. The fear was bigger than me. It consumed everything. My world. My nights. My mind.

I began to dread the nighttime routine. As the sun disappeared and the sky darkened, it felt like a heavy blanket of dread settled over my mind too. I never knew if I'd be able to sleep or if my thoughts would spiral again. The worry would start small. *What if I can't fall asleep?* But quickly it snowballed into full panic. *If I don't sleep, I'll be too exhausted to care for my son. What if something happens and I'm too tired to respond?* It was like my brain had a hundred alarms going off at once, each one screaming the same message: *Something bad is going to happen.*

And even when I did manage to fall asleep, it never lasted long. During my son's sleep regressions, the exhaustion felt impossible to bear. I'd finally drift off, only to be jolted awake by his cries. What should have been normal, expected interruptions felt like unbearable weights pressing down on me. It could take me hours to calm my mind again—only to be woken up minutes later. It was torture. I watched the sun rise so many mornings, feeling hollow and helpless, wondering when I'd ever feel like myself again—when the darkness would finally lift.

Postpartum anxiety touched every part of my life. I stopped seeing friends, too ashamed to let anyone witness the state I was in. I was a new mom with a healthy baby—wasn't I supposed to be glowing, joyful, proud? But I felt anything but. The shame was isolating. I saw how much it affected my husband too. He was overjoyed to be a dad and did everything he could to support us—caring for our son, caring for me. So many times he found me crying and would just sit with me quietly, resting his hand on my shoulder, reminding me that I was going to be okay.

He had struggled with anxiety and depression himself, so I think he understood better than most. He never judged me. Instead, he offered gentle perspective, unwavering love, and a kind of strength I didn't have in myself at the time. Looking back, I don't know how I would have gotten through those days without him.

Over the past ten months, I found myself wrestling with my faith in ways I never had before. The trust I once held in God's goodness—so solid, so certain—began to unravel. Just five years earlier, I had experienced a radical transformation. My life had been rescued from addiction and darkness, and I gave my heart fully to Jesus. I was all in—filled with a fire I thought would never go out. The joy, the hope, the certainty that God had saved me—it was unshakable.

But as the old saying goes, *faith isn't really faith until it's tested.* And in the depths of this struggle, I faced the hardest spiritual battle of my life—one that shook the foundation of everything I thought I knew about God...and about myself.

Overcoming drug addiction in my early twenties was one of the most grueling and defining battles of my life. At the time, I was drowning—numbing the pain, shame, and fear with substances that promised escape but only tightened their grip. Drugs offered a counterfeit kind of peace. They dulled the ache, quieted the noise in my head, and made me feel—for a moment—like I was in control. I lost friends. I lost myself. I wasn't chasing a high as much as I was running from the weight of everything I didn't know how to face—trauma, loneliness, disappointment, emptiness. But the escape was always short-lived. The crash always came. And with it, deeper shame and a stronger pull to go back again.

But somewhere in the chaos, I reached a breaking point. I made a decision—desperate but determined—that I wouldn't let this destroy me. By God's grace and a fierce, almost primal will to live differently, I quit cold turkey. No rehab. No tapering. Just raw grit and day-by-day surrender. The withdrawals were brutal. The mental fog, the cravings, the isolation—it felt like dying. But I didn't die. I fought hard and I thought I had weathered the hardest storm of my life.

But nothing prepared me for postpartum anxiety.

This wasn't a battle I could grit my way through. It wasn't a single decision or a moment of surrender. It was a relentless and invaded every part of my life. Fear became my constant companion. It wasn't just emotional, it was spiritual. And it felt like no amount of prayer, no number of scriptures, could touch the torment I was in.

There were nights I lay awake sobbing, crying out to God in desperation. My mind was a battlefield of chaos, and I begged Him to bring peace. I would whisper the words I used to cling to: *"You give sleep to those You love." "You see me. You know me. You know what I need."* And then, when nothing changed, I would ask: *"God, why won't You help me?"* The silence felt deafening. My anger toward Him scared me. I knew He was powerful, but in that moment I felt abandoned. I found myself asking, *The God who saved me once...can He keep saving me?*

That question haunted me.

But even in my doubt—even in my darkest, angriest moments—I couldn't fully walk away. Something in me knew this wasn't the end of the story. That this wrestling, this raw and brutal season, was still part of the journey.

Because the truth is, God's love isn't afraid of our doubt. His presence doesn't leave when we start asking hard questions. And even though I couldn't always feel Him, He was there—in the quiet, in the chaos, in the middle of my unraveling.

And slowly, subtly, that's where healing began.

# CHAPTER SIX

## Resisting the Real Enemy

*"The devil fears hearts on their knees." —Corrie ten Boom*

If you know me, you know I'm not great at keeping things to myself. I'm the type who gives gifts before I'm supposed to, who blurts out surprises because I can't hold in excitement. I've always been an open book, especially when it comes to my life and the things I'm walking through. So, when postpartum anxiety hit me, I didn't keep it a secret. I called anyone who would listen. I talked about it constantly—not because I wanted attention, but because speaking the words out loud helped me make sense of what was unraveling inside of me.

I know so many women who suffer silently with postpartum, carrying their pain in quiet shame. But for me, speaking was survival. It didn't fix everything, but it gave me something to hold onto—connection, empathy, a reminder that I wasn't alone. I had beautiful people around me—women who prayed for me, checked in regularly, brought meals, and sat with me in my mess. Their kindness was a balm in many ways. But the real shift didn't come until I met with a woman from my church—someone who had walked through her own long and painful battle with anxiety and depression.

Her name was Carol.

I had heard bits of her story before, enough to know she had faced something similar. She had lived with crippling anxiety and depression for eight years. Eight years. And during that time, she raised six children. Yes—six. I couldn't even imagine surviving another month of this, and here was a woman who had raised a family while walking through her own personal valley. What amazed me most was that if you met her today, you'd never guess what she endured. She was strong, grounded, full of wisdom. A leader in the church. A teacher at the ministry school I once attended. Her faith had roots—deep ones. I knew I had to meet with her. I was desperate.

We finally found a day to meet at a local coffee shop. I was so nervous walking in, my son in my arms, my heart pounding like a hammer. I didn't know what I expected—maybe some advice, a list of scriptures, a "you'll get through this" pat on the back. But what I got was something far more profound. As I poured out my story—the sleepless nights, the fear, the panic, the spiritual doubt—Carol sat quietly. She didn't interrupt. She didn't try to "fix" me. She just listened. Her eyes stayed locked on mine, unwavering, filled with a kind of compassion that only comes from someone who has *been there*.

When I finally finished speaking—sobbing, emotionally drained—she looked at me and said something that caught me completely off guard.

"You haven't been resisting the enemy."

*Wait, what?*

Her words hit me like a brick wall. At first, I was almost offended. It seemed too simple. Too pointed. Almost accusatory. But then she quoted James 4:7: *"Submit yourselves therefore to God. Resist the devil, and he will flee from you."*

I had memorized that verse years ago. I could recite it in my sleep. But in that moment, it pierced me. I realized I hadn't been living like it was true. I had been fighting—but I was fighting myself. I was fighting my body for not being able to keep it together. Fighting God for not stopping the storm. But I wasn't resisting the true enemy—the one who came to steal, kill, and destroy everything in me.

Suddenly, scripture after scripture came flooding back into my heart like a lifeline:

- *"Behold, I have given you authority to tread on serpents and scorpions, and over all the power of the enemy, and nothing shall hurt you."*
  —Luke 10:19

- *"For God has not given us a spirit of fear, but of power, love, and a sound mind."* —2 Timothy 1:7

- *"They that wait upon the Lord shall renew their strength; they shall mount up with wings like eagles..."* —Isaiah 40:31

And finally, *"They overcame by the blood of the Lamb and by the word of their testimony."* —Revelation 12:11

I had forgotten who I was. I had forgotten *Whose* I was. I had the authority of Christ. I had the truth of God's Word. And in all my weeping and pleading, I had never once stood up to resist the lies that were tormenting me.

I left that coffee shop a different person. Not instantly healed, not completely free—but reignited. I had nothing left to lose, so I went home determined to fight back. But this time, I would fight *the right way*—God's way.

I put my son down for a nap, went into my bedroom, and shut the door. I grabbed my Bible, got on the floor, and cried out like my life depended on it—because in many ways, it did. I wept. I yelled. I told God the truth—my truth—ugly and raw. I quoted Scripture like it was my sword because it was. I wasn't praying pretty prayers. I was warring for my mind, my motherhood, my faith.

And somewhere in the middle of that storm—sobbing on the floor, my Bible open, my voice hoarse—God met me.

That was my turning point. My surrender.

# CHAPTER SEVEN

## The Floor Became Holy Ground

"Courage, dear heart." —*C.S. Lewis*

That day on the bedroom floor didn't erase everything. I didn't rise with a sudden surge of joy or a sense that all was well. My anxiety didn't dissolve in a single prayer, and the nights didn't instantly become easier. I still had moments where the weight of the world pressed hard on my chest. But something had shifted—quietly. Not in the atmosphere around me, but in the posture of my heart. For the first time in months, I no longer felt like a helpless observer to my own pain. I had stepped into the fight. I had taken my place in the story—not as the victim but as someone who could stand. Someone who could heal.

Each morning after that, I began differently. Not with dread or defeat but with a declaration of truth—God's truth. I would walk through my home, sometimes with tears still drying on my cheeks, and speak life. Over my home. Over my anxious thoughts. Over my son. I didn't always feel brave. In fact, most days, I didn't. But I chose to speak anyway because faith doesn't require the absence of fear. It just requires that we show up anyway. And somehow, every time I did, God showed up too. He never asked me to have it all together. He just asked me to come.

As the days passed, I started to understand that this battle wasn't just about anxiety. It wasn't just about sleep or stress or hormones. It was a war for my identity. The enemy wasn't just trying to steal my peace; he was trying to rewrite who I believed God said I was. He whispered lies that I was inadequate, unstable, unworthy of being a mother. He tried to convince me I was broken beyond repair. That I would never feel normal again. But with each scripture I clung to, those lies began to lose their power. I began to remember: I was chosen. I was called. I was not forsaken.

Healing didn't look like fireworks or miracles. It looked like breathing through panic attacks instead of letting them win. It looked like choosing to laugh with my son when I didn't feel like laughing. It looked like falling asleep without gripping the edge of the bed in fear. These weren't small things. They were victories. Quiet, sacred victories. The kind of triumphs that don't show up on social media but change everything.

I also became fiercely protective of what I allowed into my spirit. I learned to tune out the noise that once made me feel like I was constantly falling short. I stopped letting comparison rob me of joy. I stopped allowing shame to narrate my story. Instead of chasing perfection, I leaned into presence. I discovered the beauty of simply being there—with my son, with my husband, with God. I didn't need to perform motherhood. I just needed to live it, honestly and surrendered.

Looking back, now I see that season not as a sign of weak faith but as the crucible where my faith was refined. It was in the weeping, the pleading, the quiet surrender where I discovered the strength I never knew I had. I learned that God doesn't prove His love by protecting us from the fire; He proves it by walking through it with us. I learned that surrender isn't defeat. It's a declaration of trust. And sometimes the most defiant, holy act of war is simply whispering, "God, I don't know how to go on, but I'm still Yours."

Before postpartum, I had never really battled anxiety. Fear was something I could rationalize or push past. But my husband had lived with it for most of his life. In the early years of our marriage, his struggle often left me confused and helpless. I tried to be encouraging—his cheerleader, his strength—but I didn't understand the depth of what he was facing. My empathy, though genuine, didn't always translate into grace. I'd say things like, "Just try to think positive," or "You have so much to be grateful for." Words meant to help, yes, but they missed the mark.

Now, I see his pain through a different lens. I've stood in that same darkness. I've felt the weight of simply trying to make it through the day, of holding it together for the sake of someone else. I've experienced what it's like to crave peace and not know how to find it. And I've come to understand that the desire to "feel better" isn't weak—it's human. But true healing rarely comes in an instant. It comes through surrender, honesty, and time.

And yes, I still had days where the shadows tried to creep back in. But they no longer had the final word. I've walked through the fire, and I've seen the goodness of God in the middle of it. That changes a person. It humbles you, breaks you, and rebuilds you stronger.

Scripture says, "We know in part" (1 Corinthians 13:9), and that has never felt more real. There were days I was furious with God. And He took it. He didn't turn away. In fact, He met me in the bathroom where I locked myself to cry. He sat with me in the sterile doctor's office as I desperately searched for answers. He whispered peace into my racing thoughts through worship songs and quiet scriptures I didn't even remember memorizing.

He was there—not just as a concept but as a comforter. Not just as a Savior but as a friend.

So, no, the floor didn't fix everything. But it did become the place where everything began to change, for the time being...

# CHAPTER EIGHT

## Here We Go...Again

*"I will strengthen you and I will help you"* —Isaiah 41:10

A year and a half passed without a single anxiety or panic attack. I was thriving as a stay-at-home mom, slowly rediscovering the joy in everyday life. I started working out again, eating healthy, and finally gaining control over anxiety. Mornings with little hands reaching for me, afternoons filled with laughter and chaos—I was present for it all. I was learning to take every thought captive. When worries crept in—as they inevitably did—I no longer spiraled. I could recognize the lie, redirect my thoughts, and steady my emotions before fear took hold. It felt like victory.

But everything shifted the day I found out I was pregnant with my second son. Just like Eve in the Garden, just like the Israelites in the wilderness, and just like the disciples in the storm, I was quick to forget all God had done for me, all that He had brought me through. This forgetfulness—so human, so ancient—did not just steal my peace, it redirected my path. It led me back into striving, into self-reliance, into emotional wandering. What followed was not a linear journey forward, but a spiraling walk—one that would expose how deeply I needed not just to be rescued, but to *remember*.

Anyone who has experienced the weight of postpartum anxiety knows that seeing a positive pregnancy test again can bring a complicated swirl of emotions. Of course, I was excited, but that excitement was quickly eclipsed by fear. *What if it happens again? How can I manage this with a toddler?*

Then, anxiety hit like a tidal wave...**again**.

I thought I was past this. I had done the hard work—group therapy, healing, finding myself again. For a year and a half, I felt steady, grounded. I believed I had outrun the storm. But it came back with a force that caught me completely off guard.

It didn't happen all at once. At first, it was subtle—lingering thoughts that wouldn't quiet, a growing sense of unease. But then, without warning, it surged. One night, I just could not rest and my chest felt tight, my heart racing, I could not calm myself down. The night was quiet, but for me it felt too loud, too fast, too much. Worst-case scenarios, to-do lists, all the "what ifs" screaming over each other.

Anxiety started consuming my thoughts, robbing me of sleep, and filled every quiet moment with dread. I couldn't stop asking myself, *Am I really capable of doing this again?*

That question became the background noise of my days, echoing through diaper changes, toddler tantrums, and the moments after bedtime. I started second-guessing everything.

Every twinge of nausea or fatigue sent my mind spiraling. *Is it normal pregnancy exhaustion, or is it the first sign of losing myself again?*

Unlike the first time, I knew the signs. But that didn't make it easier. In some ways, it made it harder—because I *remembered*. I remembered the sleepless nights filled with racing thoughts, the panic that would rise out of nowhere, the crushing weight of guilt that came with wanting to be everything for everyone and feeling like I was failing at it all. And now, with a toddler relying on me too, the stakes felt even higher.

I started to worry—not just about myself but about how my mental health might impact both of my children. The growing concern finally pushed me to a turning point: I knew I needed to get help.

This time around, I was determined to take a more proactive approach to my mental health. After a lot of soul-searching (and even more late-night Googling), I made the decision to talk to my doctor about starting anxiety medication.

It wasn't an easy choice. I wrestled with the fear of what medication might do to my brain chemistry and whether it would affect the baby. I was scared—not just of the medication itself but of what it meant to need it. But at the same time, I couldn't go on feeling like I was barely holding it together. The anxiety had returned with a vengeance, and it was stealing time, energy, and presence from the moments that mattered most.

Eventually, I decided to try the lowest dose possible. I was still so anxious about it that I even started by cutting the pill in half—

something I don't necessarily recommend, but at the time it was what helped me feel safe enough to begin. And I'm so glad I did. The medication didn't erase the anxiety completely, but it softened the edges. It made the racing thoughts manageable. It gave me breathing room—just enough space to function again.

I've since spoken to many women about their postpartum journeys. Some were comfortable taking medication right away, others weren't. What I've learned is this: there's no one-size-fits-all solution. It's whatever you and your doctor decide is the right path for *you*. No one should feel pressured—whether that's to take medication or to avoid it.

For me, it was life-changing. It helped me show up for my son in ways I hadn't been able to before. I was more present, more grounded. I even found the confidence to take on a part-time job—something I never imagined doing in the thick of postpartum anxiety.

As a Christian, I believed that if I prayed hard enough and trusted God deeply enough, I would be okay without needing medication. I thought needing medication meant my faith was weak or that I didn't truly believe God could heal me. I clung tightly to Scripture, whispered prayers through tears, and begged God to take away the panic. But despite all of that, the anxiety didn't go away. I felt like I was drowning while trying to convince myself I was walking on water.

Eventually, I had to face the truth: I needed help—tangible help. And that realization didn't mean I had failed spiritually. It meant I was finally accepting that God sometimes answers prayers through people—through doctors, therapy, and yes, even medication.

# CHAPTER NINE

*Redemption Birth*

As my due date drew closer, a new kind of fear surfaced: fear of birth itself. After the traumatic experience I had with my first son's delivery, the thought of doing it all over again terrified me. All the what if questions bubbled like a boiling pot. *What if I can't go natural, what if the epidural goes wrong again, what if I...* But this time, I wanted things to be different.

I knew I wanted to try for a natural, drug-free birth as much as possible. My husband and I hired a doula—one of the best decisions we made. Her calm energy, knowledge, and support helped ease so many of my fears in the weeks leading up to labor.

At 39 weeks and six days, I was on the verge of a breakdown, desperately trying every natural trick in the book to coax my baby out and avoid medical interventions. Then, finally, around 8 p.m. on November 18th, I started having contractions. And surprisingly...I felt excited. With my first son, I had been induced and given an epidural, so I had never truly felt what natural contractions were like. This time, it felt different—empowering.

I labored at home in the dark, in a quiet room, while my husband and son slept nearby. He checked in on me from time to time, but I mostly wanted to be alone, focused on my breath and timing contractions. I wasn't afraid; I was grounded, calm, and in control. I breathed through each wave and rested in between, saving my energy.

By 6 a.m., the contractions grew more intense and closer together. I told my husband it was time. He called our doula, Margie, and began gathering our things. When she arrived, I was deep in labor. She gently placed her hand on my back—and I, mid-contraction, managed to say (as nicely as one can in that moment), "Don't touch me." We laugh about it now, but in that moment, I was so focused and in the zone, I couldn't handle anything pulling me out of it.

Moments later, I felt an intense pressure. I shouted, "He's coming!" My poor husband, thinking I was just being dramatic, kept packing the car. Margie, however, didn't skip a beat. She handed him the phone and said, "It's 911—they need your address." My husband asked, confused, "Why do they need our address?" *Men!*

I felt the urge to go to the bathroom, and as soon as I sat down, the pressure intensified. I was crowning. I fell to my knees and started yelling, "He's coming! He's coming!" The only way I can describe it is that I entered full beast mode. I got on all fours and started making noises I didn't even know I was capable of—instinctual, primal, raw.

My husband came back upstairs just in time to see Margie spring into action. The dispatcher was on speakerphone, walking us through every step. Somehow—don't ask me how—Margie managed to flip me onto my back in a move that could only be described as a doula version of jujitsu. Within two pushes, Myles Hendrix was born.

And to top off this wild experience, he was born *en caul*—still inside the amniotic sac, which is incredibly rare and symbolic in many cultures. Margie quickly broke the sac, a pool of water hit the floor, and then she placed Myles on my chest. He didn't cry. He just looked up at me with these big, calm, brown eyes. It was surreal—like the world had paused for a moment.

Right then, the paramedics arrived and checked him over. "He's perfect," they said. I still had to deliver the placenta (**one more big push**), and then we went to the hospital for a final checkup.

Despite all the chaos, I felt nothing but peace. It was the redemptive birth experience I had hoped for—healing in the most **unexpected,** powerful way.

# CHAPTER TEN

## Learning Is Not Linear

"You don't have to control your thoughts. You just have to stop letting them control you." —*Dan Millman*

It was not long after the high of giving birth on my bathroom floor wore off. We were settling into life with a toddler and a newborn, and it of course had its challenges. You hear all the time that going from one kid to two is such a big change, but again I really had no clue to what I was in for.

I thought EZ was a tough sleeper, but man, Myles truly took the cake. This boy was relentless when it came to sleep. He would cluster feed for 45 minutes, sleep for maybe 30 minutes to an hour, and then wake up screaming. No matter what my husband or I did, it felt like nothing could soothe him. The lack of sleep became so overwhelming that I called multiple sleep specialists, desperately searching for anything that could help him sleep.

I remember one of the specialists telling me that babies around Myles' age—about five to six months—have sleep cycles every 60 to 90 minutes. Most babies sleep right through those cycles, but

Myles didn't. He was waking up every 60 to 90 minutes, night after night, for months! As we neared his first birthday, I found myself wondering, *How much longer can this go on? Will he ever sleep through the night?*

I remember trying all different kinds of sleep methods, but nothing worked. Myles was impenetrable. I started to dread going to bed because I knew it was going to be torture. My husband would step in when he could to help me. He saw my frustration and my lack of sleep affecting me. But he still had to go to work and provide for our family so I felt like it was my responsibility to be up with Myles. But it took a big toll on me.

Most days felt like I was just treading water, trying desperately to keep my head above the surface for some sort of air. I just felt like giving up but also knew giving up wasn't an option. I would remember the scripture that "God uses ALL things for good," but my flesh would scream *There's absolutely nothing good that could possibly come out of not being able to sleep.* As silly as it sounded, I meant it.

That whole year, I would get on then off medication after a few months. After having a few good weeks I thought I was doing well enough to manage everything in my own strength, only to have a sleep regression week, a super week, or six teeth coming in at once, and anxiety would creep in and take over like an unwanted guest in my mind. It felt like a never-ending roller coaster with no way off.

I used to feel incredibly frustrated with my husband when he seemed so calm—almost indifferent—while I was in the middle of a panic episode. I couldn't understand how he could be so unfazed when I felt like I was falling apart. I questioned whether he truly cared or grasped the intensity of the battle I was facing.

But recently, I've come to see things differently. For my husband, living with anxiety and depression for most of his life, in many ways, has taught him to coexist with it. He's learned, over time, that it's simply part of his story—not something to fight against every moment of every day.

I, on the other hand, did everything in my power to reject anxiety's presence in my life. I tried to pray it away, push it down, ignore it, control it—anything to make it disappear. If I could have ripped it out of me, I would have in an instant. But eventually, I had to face the painful truth: anxiety *is* part of my journey here on earth. No amount of striving or spiritual effort could erase it completely.

That doesn't mean I've given up hope. I still believe God can heal—and that He desires healing for me. But I'm beginning to understand that His healing might look different than I expected. Maybe it's not the immediate removal of the anxiety but a deeper transformation within it. Maybe the healing He offers is more lasting, more profound, and more personal than I ever imagined.

In her book *Hope and Help for Your Nerves*, Dr. Claire Weekes writes:

> *"The relief of loosening your intense hold on yourself, of giving up the struggle, and recognizing that there is no battle to fight— except of your own making—may bring a calmness you have forgotten existed within you. In your tense effort to control*

*yourself, you have been releasing more and more adrenaline and so further exciting your organs to produce the very sensations from which you have been trying to escape."*

For so long I had been clenching my fists—mentally, emotionally, spiritually—trying to control, manage, and fix what felt so broken inside me. But the more I tried to suppress it, the louder it screamed. I was unknowingly fueling the very thing I wanted to escape, just as Dr. Weekes described.

Looking back, I realize that not understanding what was happening to me—and trying to fight it with everything I had—only made the anxiety more intense. I believed that if I could just conquer it, I would win. I thought, *Once I defeat this, I'll be free. I won't have anxiety anymore.*

But in reality, that mindset only deepened my fear. I wasn't facing anxiety, I was resisting it, and that resistance made it feel even more terrifying. I became afraid *of* fear itself. I didn't want to let it happen or move through it. I just wanted it gone. And that desperation to avoid it at all costs was actually hurting me more than the anxiety itself.

Every time panic came over me, it always began with a thought—just one small, fearful idea. But instead of letting it pass, I'd latch on to it. Then, almost immediately, my body would respond—my heart would race, my stomach would churn—and those physical sensations would convince me that something was *really* wrong. That's when the spiral would begin. My mind would feed off my body, and my body would feed off my mind, locking me in a cycle I didn't know how to escape.

I don't want anyone to think that it was all bad, because it certainly wasn't. There were days when, despite only getting five hours of interrupted sleep, I felt somewhat normal. Even those small moments meant everything. I found the energy to take the boys out of the house for a walk to the park, and it felt like the greatest accomplishment. Simple things like grabbing a coffee or going to a playdate with a friend and their kids gave me a boost, as well as a safe space to vent.

Around this time, I began to notice a shift in my perspective. Instead of asking, *Why is this happening to me?* I started reflecting on how much stronger I had become since the beginning of my postpartum journey. Rather than stressing over my lack of sleep, I would remind myself, "God, You've done so much more with so much less, and I know You'll help me through today." The more my perspective shifted, the easier the challenges seemed. They no longer felt overwhelming; instead, I was holding onto Truth.

For the first time in a long while, I truly began to "work out my salvation" as it says in Philippians 2:12. I was learning to take my thoughts captive and replace them with God's Word. The Bible is like a mirror; it reflects the person God created me to be. After childbirth, I would often look in the mirror and feel like a stranger to myself. The woman I saw didn't match who I thought I was. In time, I realized I had been seeking my identity in the wrong mirror, when the truth of who I am was waiting in God's Word.

I stopped trying to control what was happening to me and instead chose to pause, surrender, and trust in His will, believing His power would sustain me. It wasn't always easy to reach that place of surrender, but I discovered that the more I surrendered and declared God's promises, the quicker peace would come.

# CHAPTER ELEVEN

## Progress Over Perfection

I believe if God wanted to remove all anxiety from my life in an instant, He would have. But in His infinite mercy, He didn't. On some days, I would let my mind wonder and question why He didn't, but I always came back to this one Truth: God was somehow going to use this struggle for good. In the book of Romans, Paul writes, "And we know that for those who love God all things work together for the good, for those who are called according to his purpose" (Romans 8:28). Wrestling with the fact that God was allowing this to happen, not just to me but for my good, was more painful than I cared to admit. In God's great mercy toward me, He allowed me to "walk through the valley of the shadow of death" as the Bible talks about in Psalm 24:4 and, as I mentioned, to "work out our salvation with fear and trembling" as Paul encouraged Timothy to do in Philippians 2:12.

Seven years ago, if you had asked me if any of this could be used for good, I would have been filled with such anger that I might have wanted to punch you in the throat. But today, I can say with unwavering confidence that God truly knows what He is doing.

In those moments when I found myself helplessly locked on the bathroom floor, overwhelmed and unable to make sense of what was happening, He was there offering His gentle, loving hand, giving me the strength to rise. When panic took over at the doctor's office and my mind refused to rest, He guided me to a postpartum support group, showing me I was not alone. And when anxiety gripped me under the vast night sky, with my body frozen in fear, He led me to a scripture, a song, or a word of encouragement from a friend—gifts of peace, reminding me that He is a good Father.

# Real Moms' Stories

Because I think hearing more perspectives and experiences in addition to mine is valuable, I asked other moms in my community who have experienced anxiety after childbirth if they would answer these five questions:

1. How did you first realize what you were feeling was more than the "baby blues?"

2. What were your particular triggers?

3. Who or what was most supportive for you during that season?

4. Did you seek professional help (therapy, medication, etc.), and if so, what was that process like?

5. What would you tell another mom who's just realizing she might have it?

The first answers are from my friend Audrey Ruiz. Here's what she has to say:

**How did you first realize what you were feeling was more than the "baby blues?"**

"I started noticing that I wasn't myself, I always felt out of place. I always felt guilty when my parents would have to step in to help me, feeling as if I didn't know what I was doing or that I wasn't 'parenting' right."

### What were your particular triggers?

"A couple days after birth, I had a lactation consultant come in and tell me I wasn't feeding my daughter right and that I would have to pump. As a first-time mom, that made me feel like I couldn't provide for my daughter since my plan was to exclusively breastfeed. So, when close family would say why don't you give her a bottle or why don't you use formula, it was always trigger because I felt like I wasn't providing enough for my daughter and I wasn't helping her thrive. Another trigger was when I fell asleep on the couch with my daughter laying on me and she rolled off. I was so exhausted with taking care of her as a single mom. Both my parents were at work. My daughter's dad was playing video games in the back room. It haunts me every day that I could've asked him to watch her while I took a nap, but I was so set on her relying on me. I wouldn't eat for days. I couldn't sleep because of the fact that I would hear that horrid sound of when she hit the floor and the silent cry she had."

### Who or what was most supportive for you during that season?

"My mom and my faith were the two big things. When I got pregnant, I was 20. Seeing that test as a 20 year old, I thought everything was over. I had lost my relationship with God. I was going out to clubs and parties. But I had finally gotten back on track when that one night happened. You *don't think it will happen till it does. I thought everyone at my church would resent me especially the pastor being my uncle! I was scared to even say anything about being pregnant. I felt like I was this sinful person walking around. I felt disgusted with myself. But once I saw my beautiful daughter, I realized God gave me her as a wake-up call. He brought this beautiful baby in the world to be my daughter. I started reading my Bible more, going to church more, not paying attention to all of the stares, worshipping and thanking the Lord every single day for waking me and my family up. My mom has been my rock since I told her I found out I was pregnant. My mom told me she never wanted to me to feel like I was a disappointment because that's how her mom (my grandmother) made my aunts feel when they had babies at a young age. My mom was there at every appointment, every false-alarm visit, and my mom was the one who I chose to have cut the umbilical cord."*

**Did you seek professional help and if so what was that process like?**

*"I unfortunately didn't seek help, but I do have the help of my friends and family who surrounded me with love."*

**What would you tell another mom who's just realizing she might be struggling with postpartum?**

*"I would tell them that they are doing an amazing job as a mom; their baby is happy and healthy all because of them and the work they put into taking care of the baby. I would also have them seek professional help even if they feel like they don't need it."*

Now, let's hear from Anjelah Johnson:

**How did you first realize what you were feeling was more than the "baby blues?"**

*"My baby blues manifested more as anger. I was annoyed and angry, and I didn't notice it until my husband mentioned that I stopped smiling at him or showing any kind of love or affection toward him. I also had DMER where I would feel an intense anxiety shoot through my body while breastfeeding. It was awful."*

**What were your particular triggers?**

*"My husband...doing anything. Even if he was trying to be helpful, my brain was just angry with him."*

**Who or what was most supportive for you during that season?**

*"Oddly enough, the source of my anger (my husband) was who was most supportive throughout it. My sister was also very helpful and my community I created online with my followers who were going through the same thing or had gone through it before."*

**Did you seek professional help (therapy, medication, etc.), and if so, what was that process like?**

*"I talked to my doctor about it all, but I decided against medication so I could keep breast feeding."*

**What would you tell another mom who's just realizing she might have it?**

*"You're not alone. This is temporary. Take care of yourself and prioritize your mental health so you can show up as the best version of yourself for your child."*

Readers, if you'd like, now you can also answer these questions for yourself here:

How and when did you first realize what you were feeling might be more than the "baby blues?"

_____
_____
_____
_____
_____

What are your particular triggers?

_____
_____
_____
_____
_____

Who or what is most supportive for you during this season?

_____
_____
_____
_____
_____

Do you think you should seek professional help (therapy, medication, etc.)? What concerns do you have about doing so?

_____

_____

_____

_____

_____


What would you tell another mom who's just realizing she might have postpartum anxiety?

_____

_____

_____

_____

_____

# Tools for Hope

If you made it this far, thank you. From the bottom of my heart, thank you! Telling my story has not been an easy one. I felt a lot of fear as I typed these words, I felt attacked in my mind as I desperately tried to articulate what was on my heart to share with you. But I am so thankful that you took time to hear my story.

I wish I could say I've completely conquered my anxiety and regained everything that has been "lost" in my life. But just last week, as my family and I prepared to fly from Texas to California to visit relatives, I found myself spiraling once again. A few days before our flight, panic began to creep in.

*What if I can't sleep the night before we leave?*

*What if I have a panic attack on the plane?*

*What if I scare the other passengers with how anxious I am?*

*What if my kids cry the whole time?*

*What if I get so anxious when we arrive in California that everyone will worry about me? I can't have people thinking I'm not okay.*

BOOM—there it is. I realize I'm not actually worried about something going wrong; I'm worrying about the possibility of panicking. Isn't that the essence of anxiety? A flood of worst-case scenarios try to convince us that something terrible is happening, even though, more often than not, we are perfectly safe. Lately, a phrase I've been repeating to myself has been a source of comfort:

"I've been here before, I've made it through before, and I'll make it through again."

One of the things that has really helped me over the last seven years in battling anxiety and panic attacks is the '5 senses technique,' also known as the '5-4-3-2-1 technique.' This method engages all five of your senses during a stressful moment, helping you stay grounded. To use it, you start by focusing on five things you can see, then four things you can touch, three things you can hear, two things you can smell, and finally, one thing you can taste. This technique has been a game-changer for me. It helped me regain focus and brought me back to the present moment, shifting my attention from my worries and fears to my surroundings.

In addition to this, there are so many helpful breathing exercises, apps, and YouTube videos designed to calm your nerves and center you in the present. Seeking professional help is one of the most important steps you can take when dealing with postpartum anxiety. You don't have to carry everything on your own. Talking with a counselor, therapist, or psychiatrist can make an incredible difference. Joining a postpartum support or new mom's group can also be deeply healing. Being surrounded by other moms who understand what you're going through helps you realize you're not alone and that what you're experiencing is more common than you might think.

It's also worth getting your blood work done and checking in with your healthcare provider. Sometimes deficiencies such as low iron, vitamin D, or thyroid imbalances can trigger or worsen anxiety symptoms. When your body is off balance, your mind can be too. Knowing what's happening inside your body can bring peace to an anxious, wondering mind. I encourage you to explore whatever works for you. Or, if you're like me, you might try them all and keep trying until you find the one that clicks.

All of these techniques have helped me tremendously, but I have to say that the Word of God has been the most powerful tool in my postpartum anxiety journey. On those really tough days, when focusing on my surroundings didn't seem to help, I would turn to the notes section on my phone labeled "Scriptures to go to when anxious" and begin reading them aloud, over and over, until I felt a sense of peace.

I'd like to share these with you now. I pray that as you read these verses, they bring you the same comfort and calm that they have brought me.

Psalm 9:10 ESV: "And those who know your name put their trust in you, for you, O Lord, have not forsaken those who seek you."

Philippians 4:6-7 NLT: "Do not worry about anything; instead, pray about everything. Tell God what you need, and thank him for all he has done. Then you will experience God's peace, which exceeds anything we can understand. His peace will guard your hearts and minds as you live in Christ Jesus."

Luke 10:19 ESV: "Behold, I have given you authority to tread on serpents and scorpions, and over all the power of the enemy, and *nothing* shall hurt you." (Emphasis added.)

Psalm 46:1 ESV: "God is our refuge and strength, a very present help in trouble."

Job 11:15 NLT: "Then your face will brighten with innocence. You will be strong and free of fear."

Isaiah 54:14 ESV: "In righteousness you shall be established; you shall be far from oppression, for you shall not fear; and from terror, for it shall not come near you."

Isaiah 54:10 ESV: "'For the mountains may depart and the hills may be removed, but my steadfast love shall not depart from you, and my covenant of peace shall not be removed,' says the Lord, who has compassion on you."

Romans 8:6 NLT: "So letting your sinful nature control your mind leads to death. But letting the Spirit control your mind leads to life and peace..."

Romans 15:13 ESV: "May the God of hope fill you with all joy and peace in believing, so that by the power of the Holy Spirit you may abound in hope..."

Believing in these promises that God has given us through His Word is probably the most important thought you will ever face amid life's challenges. I can't think of anything more powerful than a person who decides that God's promises are truth and live like it is.

The cover image of this book portrays a woman struggling to keep her head above water. She is aware of the depths of her pain, hidden just beneath the surface, and fights to stay afloat, knowing a storm is approaching. Yet, in that same moment, she remains grounded in Truth—an anchor forged through the very trials that shaped her. Steadfast in her Creator, she knows He is right there with her. She understands that the waters will rise only as high as her Father permits, and she hears Him beside her, whispering, "Talitha Koum," meaning, "Little girl, rise."

And so, we rise. We rise, not in our own strength, but in obedience to the command of the Father. With courage, we take up the armor He has given us, the armor that equips us to stand firm in the face of any storm. We set our eyes on Him—the One who is our refuge and our strength. In every moment of doubt, we remember that the God who created us is not distant or indifferent; He is ever-present, willing and able to reach out His hand time and time again, pulling us up from the deepest, darkest seas. No matter how far we may sink or how fierce the waves may be, His grip is unshakable, and His love never fails. With every step, He strengthens us, guiding us back to the surface and reminding us that no storm is too great for His power.

For anyone walking through Postpartum Anxiety, I want to say this: There is no magic cure. No quick fix. But there is hope. Healing comes in layers. It often requires confronting the lies we've accepted about ourselves and replacing them with the Truth of who God says we are. It's a journey—a sacred unraveling of falsehood and a reweaving of identity.

## Psalm 139:7-12 (ESV):

*Where shall I go from your Spirit? Or where shall I flee from your presence? If I ascend to heaven, you are there! If I make my bed in Sheol, you are there! If I take the wings of the morning and dwell in the uttermost parts of the sea, even there your hand shall lead me, and your right hand shall hold me. If I say, "Surely the darkness shall cover me, and the light about me be night," even the darkness is not dark to you; the night is bright as day, for darkness is as light with you!*

# Author Bio

Author Anjelica Williams has spent the last several years learning to turn pain into purpose. A North Texas mom of two and happily married for over a decade, Anjelica shares her story of postpartum anxiety with warmth, wit, and the kind of honesty that makes readers feel seen. Through her debut book *Giving Birth to Anxiety*, she hopes to break the silence around maternal mental health and remind every mom that hope can coexist with healing. When she's not writing or working in childcare, she's probably watching her boys on the baseball field, finding a local coffee shop, or a combination of both.

Connect with Anjelica Williams on social media:

www.instagram.com/anjelica.b.williams/

*Giving Birth to Anxiety* is published with help from
www.100xPublishing.com

www.ingramcontent.com/pod-product-compliance
Lightning Source LLC
Chambersburg PA
CBHW070856050426
42453CB00012B/2237